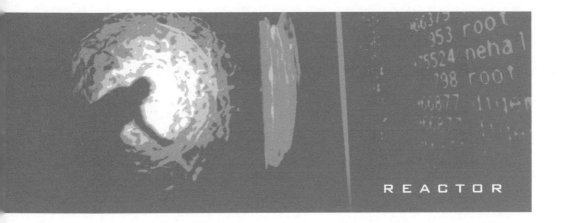

REACTOR

T0164242

THE UNIVERSITY OF WISCONSIN PRESS
POETRY SERIES

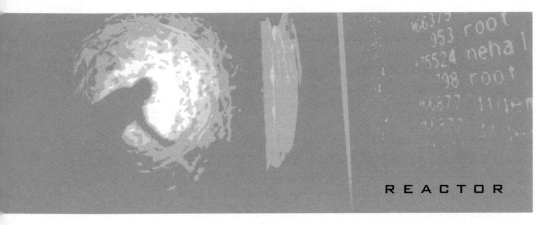

REACTOR

Judith Vollmer

The University of Wisconsin Press

OTHER BOOKS
BY JUDITH VOLLMER

Level Green
Black Butterfly
The Door Open to the Fire

The University of Wisconsin Press
1930 Monroe Street
Madison, Wisconsin 53711

www.wisc.edu/wisconsinpress/

3 Henrietta Street
London WC2E 8LU, England

1   3   5   4   2

Printed in the United States of America

Library of Congress Cataloging-in-Publication Data
Vollmer, Judith.
Reactor / Judith Vollmer.
p. cm.—(The University of Wisconsin Press poetry series)
ISBN 0-299-19940-1 (cloth: alk. paper)—
ISBN 0-299-19944-4 (pbk.: alk. paper)
I. Title. II. Brittingham prize in poetry (Series).
PS3572.O3957R43 2004
811'.54—dc22
                          2003021173

Book design: David Alcorn, Alcorn Publication Design

for
my brothers, Rege & Bob

for Betsy Kline Heltzel
and for Ed Ochester

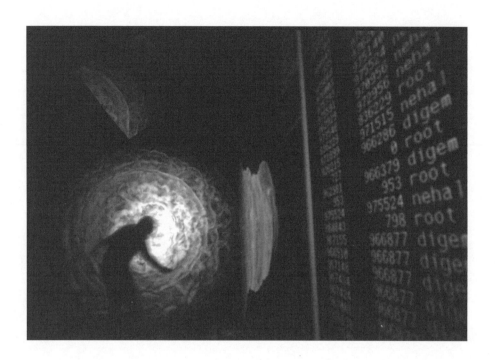

TABLE OF CONTENTS

ACKNOWLEDGMENTS

Poems in this book—sometimes in earlier versions—have appeared in the following journals, to whose editors and sponsors grateful acknowledgment is made: "The Yucca Mountain Sequencce: 'i. The Reactor,' and 'iii. U1A Tunnel: Persephone's Story,'" *Agni;* "The Coffee Line," *Crab Orchard Review;* "Spill," *Pearl;* "Note to the Mist" and "Bruche in Her Summer Kitchen," *The Women's Review of Books.*

"The Orange Sea," "Spoil Islands," "Early Snow," and "Listening to Birds after a Mild Winter" are included in *The Green Edge of Westmoreland,* a collaborative exhibition of photography and poetry, with *National Geographic* photographer Lynn Johnson. My heartfelt thanks to Lynn for her vision and companionship in the outback of the Nevada Test Site.

I would also like to thank the Corporation of Yaddo and the American Academy in Rome for residencies that provided me with solitude in which to work; and the Pennsylvania Council on the Arts for a poetry fellowship that aided in the writing of many of these poems.

Thanks to my colleagues at the University of Pittsburgh at Greensburg, in particular Norman Scanlon and Clara Vana; and to the following poets, writers, and friends whose support stands tall: Mary Taylor Simeti, Frances Baker, Diane Marsh, Richard Blevins, Lori Jakiela, David Newman, and Carole Coffee; and especially Maggie Anderson, Ann Begler, Patricia Dobler, Lynn Emanuel, Geeta Kothari, Jan Beatty, and Peter Oresick.

Finally my deepest gratitude is extended to my editor, Ron Wallace.

"Coffee with Narrative" is for Carole Coffee.
"Early Snow" is for my mother, Teena.
Thanks to April Rawluszki and Paul Vollmer for technical assistance on "The Ice Fall."

THE COFFEE LINE

The cart was a house we approached at dawn,
the man tended the chrome pots bent over
in his canvas apron, the steam a circuit above the boiling
water and the smell could knock you out at 6 in the morning;
our paper bags softened in the mist, and our lunches sealed
in waxed paper held meats & fruit—
second sweetness of the day—but this would be the first, the dark
poured into our thermoses, the dark warmed our faces
in the first-light, the smell, holy
smell of the whole oiled & turning world
smoked into our nostrils down onto our tongues,
eyes in our heads watered, ears opened
to the sound of pouring from the chrome spout,
the falling dark waterfall into the cup, 1 cup just
now before work, sipping the dark, 2 sugars, 3,
help yourself to a fourth, it's payday,
the milk warmed if possible   is that possible, the man
bends toward us hands up the cup and keeps pouring
elixir & frugality, cost & profit. Every morning
the red ring of the single burner on the white
stove in the cart can be seen from far away in the black
wet streets we walk, minds dipped in sky-tar
buffed to something ebony & bony & vase-like;
we walk toward the wedding ring of night & morning fused,
Saturn, ring of the brain's tiny volcanoes awakening.

I

For me, an object is alive.
Joan Miró
from *Selected Writings and Interviews*

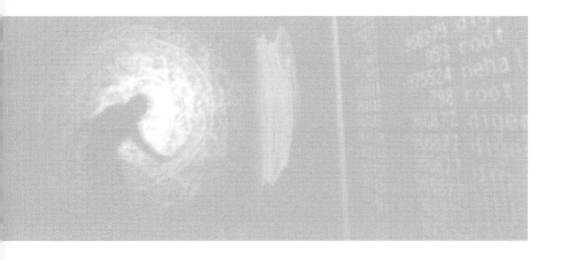

i. The Reactor

The dome of heaven was built in a single frame.
Marina Tsvetayeva

I didn't care for my brothers' toys,
even the silver cities that rose under the piano
were part of another stage. I wanted the gray tower
fitted from 500 pieces, the model someone
designed for whom, unclear; my brothers
placed it, finished, on the gameroom table,
and rejoined their camp in the woods. Someone must
know the code to its tiny red door; someone walked
its halls and polished the white floors,
the Connecticut River ran beside it,
we saw a movie on summer vacation.
Pipes big as tunnels shined plain satin steel. Something flowed
out of the tower and into the cold river
and over the bright scales of fish.
Tower with slippery sides,
dome without windows,

I studied your gray skin
then one day made myself small enough
to climb the curved ladder over the skull and down
the other side, I could see the door, the halls,
& the men in white paper suits. I took it
to school, it would be my own Taj Mahal,
palace for a princess, men in paper-white suits
would make light & heat for all the nations. My prince built the creamy white
halls for love and laid the blue tiles for the pool

of golden carp. The people would walk the graveled paths a thousand years.
Every walk a walk of sadness, yes, their princess was dead, but also
a walk of awe every day in her presence. See the swans & peach trees along
the river that flows beside it. See the terrible silver rods
& pipes filled with poison through the glass
but you never have to touch them,
the plutonium is slippery and will burn
the flesh off your hands. This is the way
we open the tiny red door and walk inside but

it was only a model after all and not the real thing the real
palace where the men stood over the silver-black pool balancing pipes the size
of tunnels and rods delicate as the bones of deer.
The princess was wrapped in her ivory skin
& black black hair braided with pearls & ribbons.
The people went to gaze into the blue water
and to imagine touching the cool fins of the golden fish.
They gathered rose petals & feathers of red & yellow birds. Dome,

slippery shell, labor of love, architect's untouchable
model, my schoolmates looked politely and couldn't see

I would have peeled you open just to see your fire.

ii. Sedan Crater, 1962–

I love this place, it is restful.

Derek S. Scammell,

ex-limo driver to The Beatles, triple-tour Vietnam veteran, & National Nuclear Security Administration guide to the proposed U.S. nuclear waste repository at Yucca Mountain; in the outback of the Nevada Test Site, October 2001

What are you breathing: pine:
Eastern white? Sugar of the Sierra
Nevada? Important to know the difference.

I have a mocha eye

There are buses at the gate, catch the diesel on the wind.
A young man is fixing his badge & the sinking feeling after donuts & coffee.

Are you breathing eye talc,
taupe silk brushed across the lid—
briefcase packed for your daily test?

A scratch of mesquite arrives in my ragged wind
Are you far

from 32 men per bus, 11 buses on their way to an elevator
deep as the Empire State Building?
Up from Vegas & Henderson the miners ride,
men of the Sheep Range & nightless casinos;
one is looking out the tinted window at beige   color no one loves
on a 2-hour ride. Before gunpoint-check & piss test

he's gazing at the curved places in the caliche:
he could crawl in
while the sun's still mild, the Sheep glint
by 8:42 sharp. He has another hour's
ride, then 15 minutes down.
Bony piles of the East, he wouldn't know you. He's carving
a new room for the silver coin of plutonium
arriving tonight in a classified white-on-white truck.

Vats of the thing that never dies,
are you far?
   Old bomb clouds
   Plumb-bob & Charlie, Buster-Jangle & Plowshare—

 —ghosts that travel the wind

I'm four football fields wide & twice that underground

A blue sky
then voices come over me

Very wide, very light here

   What are you breathing: lilac
or syringa? Random sagebrush perforate my photographed circumference

Everything you couldn't see
blasted by the switch
got sucked down

Millions
of flutes—bones, feather-stems
claws, & lungs Every creature in my range

The lizard in Mr. Stafford's poem
had to wait at the edge of the desert
trembled there

A miner can't look out a window for long,
he has to go down

Here comes the dusty start of a rain
Make a mocha cake
Make a pool
down inside the thing that doesn't die,
the dull sand-metal. Even simple coins of mica,
by comparison, glint
like cat's-eyes

And what pitch does the wind
make over me so softly?
Mojave, important
above my mocha eye

iii. U1A Tunnel: Persephone's Story

I have to keep the walls dry,
generators smooth, their nerves
are real porcupines! Keep the streets
from cracking, the sand
blows heavy above. Once I was
a woman, actually 2, in white dresses,
I lay dead, my mother wailed
over my body, then I was alive,
singing, there were gems, also
white: calcite, pearl, opal, druzy.
Now I am another.

Pipes & wire form the grid;
cable shapes the dome. Crust
protects our fortune, which is
slippery. See,
this new room painted cottage red
isn't a landfill or tomb—it's
a lab, future for the nation,
which turned, momentarily, to
Poetry, the Pope, Bono, etc.
after the last rupture. Now it's
another, too. Here's the pyro-
chiller, the diagnostic alcove.
I don't miss myself—this is home now—

and here is kismet—
lovely marine blue. Climb
the red ladder of light and
see the water for yourself. This
is the fortune.

I'm getting the hell out of here
was my father's last complete
sentence. No one laughed, no one cried,
his brain a complete mystery. I don't
miss myself—climb the red ladder,
you'll see chicken wire everywhere, familiar,
sheet rock, the pipes look like rifles,
familiar, fibre optic, steel—
easier for you, I have everything I need—
but you—

don't drink the water—
then a little window and you're
high up and out—
here's something—
let's take a sliver of plutonium and

press it under 200 Hoover Dams.
Something might happen, visually,
take that brightness with you,
a gift from this place, this city.

iv. General Brenda Gives a Press Conference

This wasn't to be on-camera—but—
                              —light me—yes, you will be escorted
to The Watermaster. Yes, the simulants will appear
                              onscreen behind me.
      ?? I'm size 12, desert cammies. Don't open that door.
Welcome, guests, to
      Area 12 Federal Camp, Preserve, & Test Site—I know,
        a real mouthful—
          fresh deer for lunch if it's not
            irradiated. We have O'Douls on ice, we're
              1350 square miles:
                size of Rhode Island: 2% contaminated,
                  98% eco-farm, national gem. Do not
                    open that door. Here we have created in 50 swift years
                      new solutions—population half a person per
                        square mile—LIGHT ME—give me more
                              volume in my mic—

Where are the Underground tests of yesteryear??
                        Retired,
                          we don't need—

      ?? Global plutonium, we own that. Yes, safest place to be in a quake—
      ?? Thermal-mechanical problems? We handle those—

We have created

     from common household chemicals

     the simulants: Israelensis & Bacillus thuringiensis kurstaki

and thus we remake the jumbotrons:

          ONE NATION UNDER GOD,

          QVC, & THE VALLEY OF THE SUN

  thus we maintain

       capability for national calamity.

     ?? I've lived long in the shadow of men . . . horseplay!

We create and preserve

  we let the deer roam

  we'll take your wastes, your Hanfords & Love Canals;

     have you noticed visual disconnects make people think?

The sight of Frenchman's Flats gives me hot flashes, sweetheart—

          Don't open the door.

Yes, I'll escort you to The Watermaster.

Yes, the color ecru is a desert pearl. We don't need—

  Simply scatter the simulants in a city and make it uninhabitable.

  We're all going to Yucca Mountain, loveys. Onscreen behind me.

?? Lo-level hi-level radioactive transports??

     We've BLOWN them UP and set them on FIRE!

     NOTHING HAS BREACHED!

?? No, no gloves or tucks, my skin is fully oxygenated.

?? Evian, yes; no,

  Bacillus globigii

     formerly used in pesticides.

Anyone with a couple million bucks in her pocket can do the simulants.

Lo-level hi-level, pores, faults, capillary action; we take your bloody waste—!

    10 years for it to percolate down to the water table—

    where it's fully absorbed

                         in zerolites—exactly like cat litter!

    ?? Yes, cover of *Time*,

                  Common household chemicals

and we can scatter

               simulant over any city, we don't need

the Bomb.

    Yes, we have vaginated peacefully

    whole territories.

    ?? What else? Liz Taylor, White Diamonds.

    ?? Our air is standard issue: thank you, the escort is here.

    Your sinuses will clear in 3 minutes.

    ?? Screw Nevada.

                    I AM THE WATERMASTER.

                                        What I'd

    like next? I'd like your pink

    doggie dick in my mouth

    is what I'd like.

v. Note & Xeroxed Letter Left in Grotto #8,
Yucca Mountain, October 2001

October 20, 1971

Dear Jude,

Eighty-four, you're old enough to go
but when we buried you
last Spring I couldn't. I found
a crooked heart growing
when the grave-grass sprouted,
and a feather once. This is a beautiful
place I'm calling *tunnel of black*
moons, but maybe you know where
you are. Some really smart kids
from Berkeley are counting
eyedroppers of water on the other
side of this wall, checking
for fractures. You'd like our guide,
John Dinsmore, who says after
the trucks come bearing it
from the rusting plants and leaching
marshlands, after the fractured
highways have to bear it, cops
escort it, guys slide it all in here,
they will button it up and walk away.
John says we need a language
people will be able to read
in 10,000 years: alien-code
for *Danger, Stay Away!!!*
The West is too big for me.
You always said "Let's get going"
when it was time to leave, darling
young father.

It's really great reading your letters
about your trip and you do such a fine
job writing that I think we should have
sent you long ago to get you into focus.
I now know what they mean by not seeing
the forest for the trees so keep up the good
work! The baseball world series are over,
and so that you know who is writing to you
I must show a bit of bigotry and say that
our blacks are better than their blacks?
At least my friend Willie thought it was
funny and the Pirate win was nice cause
your mother liked it a lot. Big Nick
returned home on Saturday and said he
hated not seeing you but he had to work
every day and didn't want to lose time going
home. A few of my friends are there always so
if you should need something sing out to
them at the plant and it will happen. Your
new family sounds so good and you are so
very lucky that you must invite them to visit
us anytime they can make it! Since I am not
going to Japan I have been assigned to the
California refueling & repair in January.
I'm glad because your mother can visit
me and breakup the winter months. I'll
only be away three weeks and then we
will start our plans for next years vacation.
It's only five weeks about since you started
your visit and although we miss you a lot
we are thrilled and are enjoying Europe
almost as much as being with you. There
is never a day that someone at work doesn't
ask where you are and wishes the best for you
because we all know that you are presenting
your best and representing us to everyone

there. My gang also thinks you are the greatest
especially the metallurgists since I showed them
your letters about rod Iron? Wrought *Iron*
as any artisan familiar with the art of metal
working and from Pittsburgh no less knows
dear daughter!! What has your father wraught?
What a waste of money, it's ENGLISH *pollution*
of our very way of life! Enough of that Jude
because we are having a hearty laugh with
you and now that I've started to write to you
I'll make it more often as I believe we can make
this world a better place if we do it together
OK? I'll take care of things here and you handle
them there by keeping us informed as we know
you will. Have fun be happy get rest, smile
and all that kind of junk but please say
thanks God bless you,

      Love XO Dad

vi. Abandoned Camp near Paiute Mesa

Out in the fallen corral

among stones a pocketful of stones

clustered in the sand: the cool

blue-gauze water of bright turquoise.

II

One seems to shed a skin or husk, once in so often—a biological
process—in fact, the whole race has got to slough off, out of it—
the past I mean—and this "new creation" is already on us.
H.D., 1943
from a letter to Norman Holmes Pearson

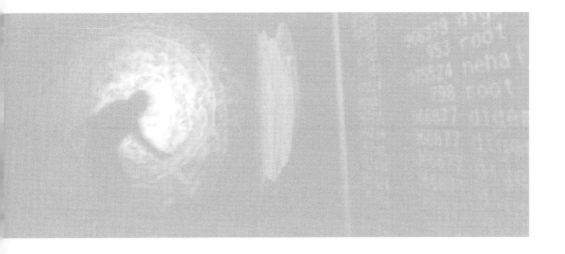

NOTE TO THE MIST

at H.D.'s grave

I belong to you,
          O nonhuman mind, scarf knotted at the throat,
               my mind's a sax, brass gone smoky.
                                        I could call you
spider web blown in from Palermo,
     but we're in a different town. Good to lunch
          on bread & sharp yellow cheese a few blocks from Bethlehem
               Steel, very good to read
     one more page of Baudelaire
                              to her,

Greek flower
     All flowers are roses,
                              even you, mist,
unfold your pearlescent lips from the black trees.
     Your shreds & veils are blocking my peripheral vision
                         but I see through you, I'm writing on you,
my blue ink's running blue.
     The December pines are still waiting for snow
      or bending for something fluctuating
     and changing colors.
          I brought thick paper for a grave rubbing, but
               your wet kiss floats me up a hillside,
          you're making the mountains bigger, closer. Which jade cloud
opened up a thousand miles north?
                         Which far waterfall
sent your organza veils?

                    When London fell around her,
when the rails were ripped out of their tracks
and melted down for guns
she thought about running away,
               on wealth, or love's vapor.

Astronomer's daughter, single mother, untranslatable
	seer, senser of vibrations on the windscreens
	that move our lives,
		behind a slightly open door

	she is sitting and practicing the hard
	facts of her vocation.
					Good when the gatekeeper
waved me in to the serpentine
	and casually pointed
	the exact pathway to her.
				Some of the men (& later women too)
hated "the American Virginia Woolf"
	for the hush of servants, the child
	ushered away from mother's study. *We all could get our work done*
		if we had that kind of money. Enough.
I belong to you,
O nonhuman mind,
I'm dissolving and oxidizing
				in the intelligence of your strange movements
that come and go in this mild air.
	When I got out of the car I was walking around in a daze
		through the chalk-white paths & matte greenways toward

this white stone   her words on it
and blood dampening my jeans, no kidding, my assumed
	last & final menses
		replicated. This morning I dreamed I was walking
along a balustrade, Pittsburgh falling all around me and
		no place for me to go
		so I sat down at my desk and worked.
Who can hold onto the safehouse of quiet work?
					Where is she gone to,
mist, little house of silver pencils, little Grappa bench I sit on,
gray day like a porch
		sandpapered down to wood grain,
to skin, to the fire inside me?

It was coming down hard so the teacher motioned the flute
then the piano quiet and the children sang

a cappella, teacher's voice was gone, they screaked and worked
their lungs & shoulders like gulls, they swooped and cranked

it up, it was wonderful being all alone,
they could hear pauses, one by two by one, then she

ran to the edge of the world, opened it and thrust the dark
sleeve of her dress out & down into the whirlpools

and when a flake landed crisp & complete on the black
wool she ran to every desk then back for more until

she showed every voice a new jewel, an alien, autotelic
shape. What would you like to be, or who, or would you

go with the wind sweeping the parking lot & small bank of trees.

Spoil Islands

waste fills off the Atlantic shoreline

With the wild birds I slipped into gliding, a tiny ceiling of feathers, I crossed
and fell to the dunes, my fingers brushed the cattails, velvet columns marking
the temples of the shallows. How I twisted in the strands of plastic & grease,
and among the young sea-oats splaying their gold straw I grazed the thou-
sand white mallow flowers that fade—white lies—so quickly no eye records
their delicate paper skin, silk after the waxy flesh is gone. I thirsted for
rainwater in the green plates of sea grapes, I loved the blossoms waving their
shreds of batiste in the southerlies, holding up little flags even as they
bloomed, died, bloomed. My shadow on the tips of new leaves was released;
it stood at the lip of the sound, my eyes slid under the cleft of a hillock, eyes
cooled the sun-hot wires of a bridge-span. How I trembled over the flowers
again, but wanted to lie down on the original sponge & bed—gone—stitched
now with ground glass & benzene, blue myrtle & wet grass. Great translu-
cence, however long 10,000 years or 10 times that, great silt, great ourselves,
little depots of grit & shifting light.

Voltaire's 70 cups to my 2,
what does that make me, though
his we think were demitasse and mine
are big as small dogs. How no one
smokes anymore, sad, I open my pack
here in the night kitchen and out comes
the exotic Mlle. Teuer, laughing, black cat
on her shoulder, and I rivet on her cup
of sugar-tar while she smokes into the night
and regales me with her vanished minor opera-
star years, drops of holiness wetting her smock.
If I run my hand along this shelf I slide into a farm-
stead where I drank the green, the black teas,
organic leaves picked from bushes silvered under
rain in far places no longer far. But the beloved sister
to merlot & cognac, to mountain water over matching
ice cubes would be the gift of Ethiopia
that would transmogrify Earth.
Dear red berries who made goats dance about,
dear leaf veins standing turgid & erect, how
the little goats in their happiness peed
on those bushes, thus deepening the primal
blend from Dante to Beauvoir;

books are wires & nerves lined up and tangled
in the starry intelligence of our evolution:
Achievement in American Poetry/Miss Bogan
praised our young literature grand as
Interstate 80 running East/West through
the basins & ranges the woolly mammoths ran,
rockfaces a thousand tints of gradation. This
road trip packs thermoses & olives, round

& square cheeses, paints, sheets, towels,
& friends, not tidy aesthetes:
"The natural voice is dead."
"Accessibility is a myth."
Birds zoom down to the Bluegrass following paths,
might reincarnate, might not, humans will
eradicate them, might not.
The experiment occurs
and I am the experiment.
Dickens got meta-psyche 100 years before Barthes:
"*I* know your tricks and your manners," said Jenny Wren.
    "*I* know where you've been to."   I got Marx
on uneven development
because a nun who was mean hungover
spelled it out in plain English. Literature is deadly.
Before I knew it Calvino slipped a needle-
story into my vein, scalding & doubleblack.
An experiment occurs in a vessel:
a young man wearing new chinos curled into
a coffin-sized pipe in 1952
and manipulated the plutonium.
"Make this fail-safe," he prayed,
tho the poison kills for generations.
Genius is (partly) in the tools: the human eye
sees 60 million colors, the rest is usually a story.
For years I never tasted coffee. I liked
staring at the dented silver pot, I liked
watching the water turning dark
inside the little glass dome.
Was my mother mannish or glamorous
sipping from her china cup? I was up
all night writing a paper for my sister
on *The Satin Slipper* and O the combination
of Claudel & the coffee filled me with absolute

euphoria. Words toss in their sleep
and gather radiance, Ovid scribbles
a sentence and turns exile to gold.

Across the sea a Bristol girl writes of blood
in the eye of a stray. She will clean and feed
it, lay it in a sheepskin box
until it sleeps itself healed, stroke its
black paws & white throat-necklace and it will be
her Coco Chanel of cats, dancing and leaping
for the foil ball. The summer I made
a strange series of exits, everyone thought
I was bereft, without love; I was, I couldn't
hear The Sirens, those eyelined
intellectuals chatting at the sidewalk
tables, so in-the-moment. I was the silver locket
at that one's throat, I was the brown disc inside
that one's cup, resin of gorgeous night. I couldn't
stop slipping into a new skin. How would I
recognize myself? I am the experiment! I
was a human walkway gliding through a copse
of sycamore, dizzy constellation of something
I was trying to forge from stars & dust.
When I woke up in Pennsylvania
it was Italy, it's no different,
we grow things, we've got woods & rivers.
But Roman terra-cotta is unique, and
we make perfect butter. But the vases unearthed
at Blue Mesa bear both tipi emblems & marks
of Crete! Original or derived, collaged or washed,

the clear work of a human hand is true. The Euro
looks best in Italy, raised streets incised on the coins,
loggia perfumed with roses & cedar,
city planning meets your eyes every time you buy a *doppio*.
My Baci poured me a cup of hot milk and then
into it poured a cup of hot coffee.
Every summer evening she scattered the day's
grounds under the roses,
they bloomed for 50 years. I
bled a bloody heart of Jesus for love, an old story,
but it was new to me. The story we must tell

we tell. I've become an anglophile
this Spring Break, learning to write
by pushing a pram around London. I find
Woolf, except for *Lighthouse*, rather a bit thin.
I like pre-writing, housework in general,
as now I'm digging dirt from the kitchen tiles
with my fingernail. This dark shining morning,
on the other hand, I'm traveling
light or, you could say, free.

On Reading a Fragment from Nuclear Safety Commission Files Explaining the Events of June 30, 1918

One afternoon in high summer
in brilliant sunshine,
in Siberia,
from vast forested
Tunguska,
a radius of sound
rang 600 miles.
The column of fire

could be seen 250 miles away
despite blinding sunshine.
A sudden
natural disintegration
occurred.
Simple uranium shifted under Earth's
crust and collided
or united
with something else
completely natural.

No, it was not a meteorite,
nor was it a human war,
no fragments were ever found.

Something natural
yet inexplicable, happened,
in brilliant
high summer
in Siberia.

VALERY LARBAUD (1881–1957):
IMAGES

an imitation

One day in Karkov, in a working-class neighborhood
in the Russian heartland
where all the women wearing white shawls on their heads
look like Madonnas
    I saw a young woman coming from the fountain,
    carrying as women have since Ovid
    two buckets suspended from the ends of a stick
    balanced on her neck & shoulders. A child in rags
    walked over and spoke to her, and she tilted
    to the right, leaned, and set the bucket down
    so it rested on the ground,
    level with the lips of the child who'd kneeled to drink.

And one morning in Rotterdam,
it was September, about 8,
I watched two girls saying goodbye
    at one of the great iron bridges,
    going off to work in separate directions.
    They kissed and held hands
    while they gazed into each other
    and held each other, motionless, inside the dizzy web
    of commuters while tugboats grumbled on the river
    and trains whistled and maneuvered the bridges.

    Between Cordova & Seville
    there's a small station where, for no known reason
    the South Express always stops.
    You can strain your eyes
    for a village sleeping under the eucalyptus trees
    but all you'll see is the Andalusian countryside, green & golden.

But on the other side of the track, facing it,
there's a hut of black branches & earth.
At the sound of the train
a clutch of ragged children comes out,
their older sister leads and approaches the platform.
Without saying a word, but smiling,
she dances for pennies.
Her feet in the dust look black;
her stained dirty face isn't beautiful.
She dances, and through large holes
in her skirt the color of ashes
you can see the slack flesh & movements
of her skinny thighs & her little
yellow stomach, rolling.
This is why, every time, some men laugh
in the odor of cigars in the diner.

postscript to a god:

Will it never be possible
for me to know that sweet water-woman
    there, in the lost home of my own ancestors,
& the two Rotterdam girls
& the young beggar dancer,
    and for me to bind myself to them
    in indissoluble friendship?
(They won't read this poem, they won't know my
name or heart; but they exist;
they're living *now*.)

Will it never be possible
for me to be given
the great joy of knowing them?
I don't know why—my god—but it seems
that with these four
I could conquer a world.

*an imitation**

LYING UNDER AN ARBOR WHILE DREAMING OF THE SEA

My body was sad and I'd read all my books.
I wanted to eat the basket of grapes then take off
for turquoise waters & beach-glass hieroglyphs at my feet,
for an indigo ribbon horizon. Goodbye for the nth time,
sorrows, I said, and I sucked the brightness from those grapes,
I lifted the empty cluster to the sky, laughing, drunk, I inflated
the shining skins and looked through them till dusk. Nothing,
not even the old gardens my lover's eyes reflect, not even
the night-talk his ebony coffee ignites, unpacked me. I was
gone, the bees turned my head in circles and all circles
lead to the dizzy sea.

* *includes lines from "The Afternoon of a Faun" and "Sea Breeze"*

Off night-trick, off double-overtime no pay, here now in Rome my dead

uncle & father begin a gradual stroll down, and enter.

"*Wow, built like a brick shithouse,*"

Uncle crows, walking in circles under the shadows of Heaven.

Built by Hadrian to last, the oculus

is a miracle in a thunderstorm: drainage holes in the marble floor.

Dad in shirtsleeves walks the perimeter among the pagans & saints.

Face wet with spring, he looks up through the black hole:

"*He was a smart man.*"

Fort, stone dome, church, temple—

My table umbrella creaks under the drenching May rain,

and the fountain musicians, the bride & groom, sing

on inside the crush of tourists heading down & in.

A Vietnamese girl sells scarves that faint in the mist of beautiful dollars & lire.

"From my town, Puglia, one rarely gets to Rome," the waiter says,

pouring water & wine. "Berlusconi & Bush, the newspapers shout, yes,

the *dolce vita* very alive in the North, 20% unemployment
in my Southern home."

Once long ago at the Fermi plant up North

when my dad & uncle were Americans 20 years after

the War, working six weeks in a town called Santhia,

not far from the silkshops of Como

Uncle hoisted a VW beetle because he could, he was

Big Nick, and the Italians loved it every night in the parking lot

after work. Dad told it a hundred times, acted it out,

the lifting of the rear bumper and tilting the Bug and pivoting it 360

full circle all the way. Bottles of red passed all around. Ghosts all,

dreamers all, stroll down into the stone house where dreams are made.

III

... the mouth full of grapes and the bodies like loose leaves.
Gary Snyder *from* "Night"
No Nature: New & Selected Poems

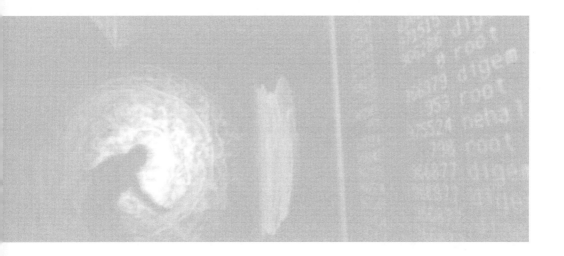

PERSEPHONE RETURNING

You come

pressing in through the fresh washed screen

this mild evening when

I haven't lit the new candles yet. But come

in, I can feel your atmosphere, dense, wet,

a field-lake let loose; a moment ago I noticed

something on the dark slate under the vestibule light.

It looks like sweat

almost a wet moonglow

pressed there   a woman's cheek fresh with night

I think you made a simple turn in the meadow last November:

could've been any

joyous-reckless one of us.

I am still asking:

is there a world before self-consciousness binds us up?

I'm still trying to be—say it—

the person *making*.

Once I liked writing

as if I were playing the piano.

Then at one point I did not want to translate the notes;

so they went directly into my hands.*

When I can't hear myself think

I watch for your comings & goings.

I bring the outside in. Moon

for light. White birchbark for sleeves.

*This quotation is from the notebooks of photographer Francesca Woodman.

THE DEAD LUCIA

for Guy Rossetti

In the September kitchen she stands straight
in her slip, one strap slips its peach satin down
the curve of her shoulder, she washes plums,
their sugar turns purple-black in the oven
and when the pies come out they're dark &
syrupy, beautiful to handle and place on the table—
company's coming—slices of heaven will drip down
chins, hands, arms up to the elbows. Lucky,
plums disappear overnight, a stranger passes
in the street and takes them in a sack,
kids tear them down for a throwing game.

I walk up and down the alley picking up plums,
carry them inside in my apron, bruised, I wash
them here in the sink, I can hold five in the palm
of my hand before my fingers knot up. Plums are
different from peaches, they're fleshy, animal &
meaty, alive as Saint Lucy's eyes. She plucked
her own eyes and laid them on a silver platter,
or was it a mirror? I loved her black hair
wrapped around her neck, in a picture my mother
had, my mother's name, Lucia, and light where her
eyes had been. Handed those eyes over, she was
mad! I imagine her eyes could see through those
men, they could probably see through walls.

35

Come down
to her stone cellar
round as a jug of water;
it is singing:

Bushel of plums in the doorway
Bushel of plums for free
Someone left them for me
I love them all
The ones with spots, pecked by crows
Tiny ones picked too soon
Tart-skinned, almond-stoned
September plums for free
In the morning doorway

She stands straight on a clean floor
over a sinkful of plums,
counts, slices each one into sliver moons,
presses them onto the dough,
round & round
in pearl light

Then sparkling sugar rains down on those moons,
and into the oven the pies go;
plum-smell brightens then caramelizes the room,
the poured glazing tints the walls
apricot & currant.

THE MOON REPLIED

I asked how the moon could be imperfect—
it's up there in heaven! How could it be mere
gray rock when its reflections prove
it's made of many translucent layers?
and how could it, old mirror,
give me no answers.

anonymous, fifteenth century

Look at old walls after they've crumbled:
now look at the patina—see the battles, animals,
see they're only stains.
Now lie down and in the deep of the night
give shape to your brilliant day—you've seen
human brains; they look like a breathing mass
of gorgeous snakes! Let that be

an invitation to wander with me.
My markings & grazings, you didn't know
what they were for 4,000 years.
So now you know
and it doesn't matter so much,

I'm still loony. I'm still a circle cut from a gray satin dress.
My scratches where landings dragged their gear
are only human. My dead oceans give me the kind
of character you surely recognize:

Look at yourself, you have the long nose & weak vocabulary
of a minor Dickens character, but basically
you're a relatively handsome modern woman.
Barnacles, coves, craters, I could give you

an earful of citations:

"Some said I was unknowable as the ocean."

"A fearsome planet that could cause a tidal wave all on its own."

But I'll just tell you:

I've created a dozen landscape effects at most,
and mostly with my dimmest rays—

As for answers, you already know
my strongest rays get lost
in lovers' eyes.
Now sleep with me behind this silver cloud.

AFTER READING THE VERSES OF
A GREAT AMERICAN POET

all that was left of me was a stick
lying on the floor, a beautiful stick,
it was golden tan, it must have come
from an old sacred poplar grove or a
young gleaner's stack, weathering,
it had my bony forehead
& long fingers, it even had
my initials burned into it
because that is what the poems did to me
burned me into wood tossed
and rinsed by the sea.
I was light enough to toss myself
around the room, the window was open
and the tips of the pines moved. Up
in the treetops winds swirled me
onto a fresh green spool, I spun and I drifted,
my fall was swift & painless, I tumbled
and unwound, I rolled over sidewalks and slid
through the black teeth of a grate,
what I saw down there! I was a new citizen,
I spoke languages and carried a beltful of
golden keys, the doors were huge
but not one creaked at my entrance,
I could be used, leaned into a firestack
with other sticks, I could hardly wait till
somebody lit the match and I burned

THE ORANGE SEA

the iron in runoff from old mines
often stains streams orange

Robert, my younger brother, lashed 4 boards
to 2 Dodge tires to sail your currents
& sour mist. He stayed your banks
with meadow rocks
and set camp under your willow:
beans, lantern, jerky, soup.
He wandered your crayfish caves
and slunk home at dusk, stained orange

and wearing your greasy necklace.
He sleepwalked to the window to gaze
across the white pines that ran
down to your rushing waters.
Washdays our mother lifted his clothes
with an old barbecue fork,
he was her last, her baby, but

you, initiator, dipped him in sludge,
molded his boots with burning muck
and rusted his zipper off its track.
    You, did you know
    where you came from in the dark,
    busted open for a few veins of coal,
    mighty you,
    though Sulfur Creek
    was the only name we knew you by.

I've never prayed to saints.
Sometimes to my dead parents.
Once to a waterfall when they took us out West.
Bake a pie from scratch, that's a prayer.
You know, the house, the temple.
Soon as I started seeing the fox down in the park
I saw it almost every evening last summer.
My first friend was Louise Williams.
She lived up by the Singer Mansion and gave me
my first cup of oolong tea. And that four-foot cactus
I still have. She taught me to graft roses

and she canned five shelves full of yard fruit
every year. She took care of us all
the year I had the twins then lost
my mother. When your father dies, it's a knife,.
but when you lose your mother
the moon goes away. My mother would never
imagine I have two kitchens, one just for
summer, the heat goes right out these big screens.

Imagine, in the middle of town:
dead train tracks, broken buildings,
& a spring-fed creek you washed your car in.
If you haven't seen what happens
to a small American city that dies—
or changes—where everybody in town
knows all and has always known all—
you've seen nothing. You know how lonely
when you start remembering: all the lost people
out on porches.

The men on the bridge might not be men,
they might be boys glazed hard & bleached out.
They slouch like wiry rock techies. This is all a show
this is no show   They might not stand up to time, to work
the way some paintings can. They're too easy. Who are they.

                Some drop
coins into the cup of the one I'll call the lead.
He cursed me last week as I passed, blank. Then I saw the dogs.
They lie in dead sleep while the lead & his men hold the bridge.
He's working, asking every single person he can for money.
Today I stopped. There was only 1 small dog,
there had been 4. Where are your dogs, I said.
This is the only one we have now, he said.
Did the others run off? Yes, that's what happened.
His eyes were wet blue. He smiled a vacation breeze.
I felt a hole in him 10 feet deep.

            The dogs sleep
like the dead, heads down, paws & tails out
slack exactly because they are up all night
keeping guard over these boys who feed them
run them ragged.

The President of the United States today proposes drilling Yellowstone for
oil. Beside me in an alley near the Via Garibaldi a man is balancing a
squeegie & a crutch, bending over his scooter, wetting the sponge from the
dripping mouth of an ancient bronze wolf. He polishes the windshield-eye
under the Roman May noon, the water tastes cool & slightly metallic,
slightly oily, rich & full as the finest olive oil born of green & silver groves.
Dogs, babies, birds in cages, women in suits & spikes stop at the wolf for
big deep drinks. When wolves returned to Yellowstone, most Americans
were happy about it. When a woman in California was mauled by a cougar
while jogging I think most felt she was unfortunate and were saddened, but
others said it's time to hunt cougar again. When coyotes started running over
north central Pennsylvania, the hunters salivated and some of my cousins
started shooting bobcats, though they remain endangered. Here the beloved
cats sip at the basins, and clean water still runs down from the Janiculum.
Last night walking down by the Tiber I hesitated, not knowing or unknow-
ing what makes grief so big.

Not far from the wolf sits a temple of Minerva buried under a church of
Catherine of Siena. Catherine's remains are there, and so is the young
Michelangelo's Christ carrying the cross. Down by the river last evening the
small cities of boards, plastic, & glass bottle lamps were awake. Albanian &
North African kids, families, were sleeping under the simple reflections of
cars passing above. The sewage system down there is the slap of the Tiber as
it meets the city wall. Some wounds heal. Every fountain says I give you
youth & wealth.

Streetlights out again I'm walking in the dark
lugging groceries up the steps to the porch
whose yellow bulb is about to go too, when a single
familiar strand intersects my face,
the filament slides across my glasses which seem suddenly
perfectly clean, fresh, and my whole tired day slows down
                              walking into such a giant thread
is a surprise every time,
though I never kill them, I carry them outside
on plastic lids or open books, they live
so plainly and eat the mosquitoes.
                    Distant cousins
to the scorpion, mine are pale & small,
dark & discreet. More like the one
who lived in the corner of the old farm kitchen
under the ivy vase and behind the single
candle-pot—black with curved
crotchety legs.
            Maya, weaver of illusions,
                how is it we trust the web, the nest,
                the roof over our heads, we trust the stars
                our guardians who gave us our alphabet?
                We trust the turtle's shell because
                it, too, says house and how can we read
                the footprints of birds on shoreline sand,
                and October twigs that fall to the ground
                in patterns that match the shell & stars?

I feel less and less like
a single self, more like
a weaver, myself, spelling out
formulae from what's given
and from words.

To de Beauvoir after Reading One of Several Fashionable Pathobiographies

One removes the trash as one removes
a mouse carcass—no, the smoking head of a horse—
no, this one's a jackal,
it feeds, slinks. The blood's delicious,
the neck bones so soft.
You weren't nice, you couldn't care, you knew

if we are who we sleep with
(or don't), we're all fucked.
Odor of the shrink
in the text I just dumped: it wasn't you
the bleeding hack cared about: and surely not

your blinding work that taught us how to think:
it was herself, self, valise so pretty
& neatly packed, she missed the screaming train.

wrapped & close & fragrant
in her incense of strange lemon soap.
She carried me down, all the way down
into her solitude, lace & bones was all
she was under the t-shirt
faded to watered black silk, thin
as her night veils, dreams

of wet earth, spring, Amsterdam
where she hung with the houseboat boys,
loading bricks of blond hash safely on;
she nursed their sore throats with concentrations
of aspirin & oranges. Spent her money on
artcards & books with blue wrappers.
Whores in windows moved
their lips like bright candies
and petals drifted down

onto my dark woven shoulders
& the three weeks we had,
hotels, of course, also her parents'
canal-side perch where I held her
while she read her Stendhal, her Colette,
the stitches of my devotion
weight she counted on
for *quiet, let's find the exact point of focus, now that's desire,*
isn't it? O it is sex, mother
of all creative energies, books, & companion views.

I liked her
in the cool air of her balcony nights.
I was left on a train and once in a musty café.
I was handed down, yes, but never
taken up so fondly.

Jan would like to be
a twin,
I want to be a bed.
The city's iced over
this spring equinox
and we're hatcheted
by our jobs; caffeine & sugar
can't help
so we toast health: spinach & eggs,
15-grain bread. Maybe if you learn
to cook eggs this good, Jan,
Don will take you to Paris, I say,
tilting over the stove. She growls
"Yeah," but her twin
buys the sex-toy Harley
and smears domesticity
on the asphalt. Mystery is alive
under our feet. Something's boiling
up to the green level. I'm nothing
but a calendar, I need
to be more like the shifting sands, I say,
no, a bed on the ocean
held up by a thousand people's hands,
without the people. "I'm going global
with my radio show,"
Jan says; "I'm gonna kick ass, take up more space."
I'm a desert rat
wasting in its midden, I say,
repeating that blokey Brit word:
midden. I never got over
the British Invasion & wearing white lipstick, I say.
"Sometimes I miss getting high," Jan says.

I miss all-night
fucking, I miss traveling around
on five dollars a day, I say.
I bought a ten-dollar dress yesterday,
I say, it's dark blue & vintage
and feels really good on.
"You have to stay ready &
wet, you have to stay open,"
Jan says, "Need & desire."

JULY EVENING WITH ANCESTORS

Narrow & green under the summer canopy
my daydream calls up

a sea turtle dozing on my lap so I can study
its shell, ancient model for the igloo,
a nice idea in July

and a boy streaming the hard reverb
of his black stratocaster onto the quiet street,
the hard pure sound
breaks the sauna air a little

and now a canal
tinted & flavored by gardeners &
cooks taking smoke breaks and pausing
to snip the wild mint.

The canal darkens, also,
with hands slipping sandals from tired feet,
and brightens
at each footbridge with sconces,
slender guides that light-finger the shadows.

IV

I once saw a hand-cart being pushed through the street and on it was a huge mirror in a gilded frame. The greenish evening sky was reflected in it and as I stopped to watch while it went past I was feeling extremely happy, and I had the impression that something important had happened.

Natalia Ginzburg
from "My Vocation"
The Little Virtues

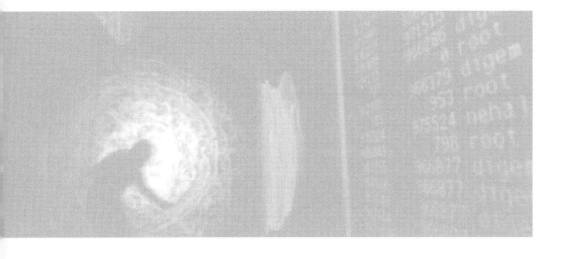

    The world breathes
its generous display: You can have this! And this!
Look mama, a fish tail! a child cries at the icy
seafood window, and in the blip before hearing
her mother's *Yes!* she's gone, time
is silk, burning, eyes out of nowhere open petals, pages
—she's through, she's peeking
onto the tip of the flat-wavy universe,
a world rushes forward and up through
her feet, palms & fingertips.
Ecstasy
move us, each first time.

EXTENDED FAMILY GENEALOGY

It is better to be bored at home than go
ballistic in someone else's space.
Andrei Codrescu

Today I learned from the Ellis Island Web site
my Baci's boat left Europe from Antwerp not Gdansk
which means she made a long overland journey
that remains unrecorded. My mother does not know

her own grandmother's name or town of origin.
My grandmother traveled with a two-year-old
girl not her own, entrusted to her by a lady.
Onboard she ate for the first time a banana, unpeeled,

in the company of the child, Janina,
& corpses to be buried after the Ellis docking.
Literate at home in Krakow, she never learned English
and for 40 years kept the peace & quiet of our house.

One of my favorite poets, Li Po, was descended from
Turks. Maybe his dizzy mountain airs
offer us voyages uncharted still. My mother

is named for either Marie Antoinette
or Maria Theresa, and her maiden name,
Gunia, means horsehair in Polish but also holds origins
in Palermo whose murky radiance I have begun to trace.

My parents named me for Saint Jude, patron of hopeless
causes. I have lied, cheated, and stolen. Grieved much
of it but do we ever finish. I love stealing,

not only the Desnos/"Hammock" theft,
but also the grand larceny of "The Jewel," lifted

from Cold Mountain while reading
the translations a hundredth time. (Not

theft, it's riffling, sampling!) My affinity
with the poet Larbaud is unmistakable.
Consider too my Muir-like fevers:
when only 14 he rose at 1 A.M.

to spend 4 hours reading before returning
to work his father's Wisconsin fields.
I claim my own and they claim me, certifiably.

My most famous blood relative, my aunt
who died a prostitute in Steubenville, warned
of the uselessness of fixed identity: "Honey, it's like that
black coat of yours: collects everything but men & money."

SPILL

Before, I spoke of clear things,
shadows on white tile, men in paper suits
mopping the radiated water with Kotex pads
trucked in through the security dock, 1960. Now
I see blurry grasses swaying in dusk, the starless
sky & vaporous shapes of a Pennsylvania
town behind wire fences, there in the misty
place beyond the woods. I hear a truck
sputtering with cheap gas, and boot soles
slapping cement. *Is that my Uncle Ray*
running toward the truck, away? No, he's inside
with his men cleaning the burning place
protecting the core. Dawn is a swollen eye
they work toward. Those must be cattails
waving over the marshland, those must be geese
making that slapping leather sound of flight.

Paper comes from trees, wine comes from the grape,
I love my country. Today came in two distinct parts

instead of one vat of moments. In the first part
I read without interruption of any kind, and in the second

I had time to think through some things. Like you,
all the writers in America have been looking for their fathers.

You'd like this view: white mist over the Adirondacks.
Fly-fishermen wade the dark blue Ausable,

first day of season. Beginnings: the idea we stay in love with.
I looked at the "new urbanism" photos down in the city; impossible

to know if the streets are dead or living; Eugene Smith is better, so
is Stieglitz, *a kind of old American Socrates*. And the small retrospective

of Souso-Cordoso, exiled in '44, whose masked fantasy-rabbit leaps
through sci-fi foliage & monstrous pools: nature weds technology

and survives, forever camouflaged. *Now there are a lot of things
that artistically speaking I know I could* make work. *But this no longer*

means anything to me. There's war in Algiers again,
kids & their mothers are pulled through doors and slaughtered.

I wish I knew the small inn you visited up here in the North Country
in 1946, I would take flowers . . . *the simplicity of the room, the remoteness*

of everything, make him decide to stay there permanently, to cut all ties with
what had been his life and to send no news of himself to anyone. I like working

in this cabin along the river, writing near water: plenty
& lack, Earth's greatest mystery. Hiking this morning I wanted to

lie down in the Ausable and turn into a blue-green plant,
tuning out the *Me*s. I brought your journals—one new, the other my old

undergrad copy, ink-stained & scratched with my embarrassing
margin notes: "the advance of art and empowerment of women

would end all war." My brutal country grows more isolate & frenzied,
we have all these demons: 1) cannot connect to social transformation

because money is oxygen; 2) oxygen supply visibly controlled by top 3%.
In '46 you were little more than half my age now,

though you've always seemed—forgive me—
like my slightly older brother: moody like me, in love with the sea

& wandering in a mildly delirious loneliness. As you've noted,
in America we tend to wear anticipated tragedy like a badge.

Some are drowning, some are sleeping. Enraged mirror-portraits
of our own kids keep showing up in faces of the young

all over Earth. *This big country, calm and slow. One feels that it has been*
completely unaware of the war. You were exhausted, touring,

happiest shipboard, dark & serene staring out over the water.
I've mastered two or three things in myself. The rockshapes out my window

make good company, the spruce winds are astringent.
I'm sitting by a fire and finally, who I am, another question not worth

answering. It has rained all evening. My cabin smells of balsam.
The wine carries a deep ruby color and is delicious.

Italicized phrases and sentences are from Camus' American Journals.

LISTENING TO BIRDS
AFTER A MILD WINTER

               I don't even
know where they were or if they went
far   where they slept but I think they must be
wildly happy squinting in the brightness even though
all winter my neighbors stuffed their tall fat feeders
with blobs of suet big enough for wild dogs   I don't think
they dream in color or even see it: don't they follow
shadows & charcoal slashes   Don't they ride wind-
gliders over bushes   Here's some moldy straw
Here's human hair on an open window-sill
plus worms are coming up to aerate a little
Who knows, a couple thousand night crawlers
might arrive in a gardener's truck or slide off a
boat down by the river, off hooks, half-eaten
or maybe regenerating after fishes chomped
them half off   they might end up here
only to be snatched by the lousy crows
barreling up from the park like intuition
Jays & cardinals are coming out of their REM
sleep too   The crow on the storm drain's
screaming   Get to work   the whole sky's
barking   Just because they didn't freeze
on icy twigs or get knocked over by blizzards
& drifts, they're excited

THE EAVESDROPPER

Never mind the soup is perfumed
with rosemary, her favorite, the wine
golden, this mother/daughter hour
rare—no, the folks a table over
smear their bread with soft cheese,
hold forth on their travel, stocks,
ailments—the talkers have her.
The tilt of her head calibrates so
perfectly she hears about 51% of
my story, turns to me, smiles.
Maybe the world takes shape

around her & the quick earshot
of strangers while I drift
across my projector screen to the sublime
and listen hard at the distance,
the visual ricochet of the curtains
repeats the machine-made cutwork
of the tablecloth. Through the curtains
the street washes itself

with light, whole bamboo slats,
whole butterflies of it. The street
refreshed now, is the Great Plain of January,
across which interplanetary lenses

shift, the plain could be tectonic
and shift any second now sideways—
it all comes in sideways—that bike
maneuvering over cinder, I know
that sound, I teethed on that crunch,
delicious black cookie on the teeth.

I can't hear without looking,
look what she's missing, but pretty soon
she will have taken the table world
fully inside and will recite it verbatim
in the car, later, so in this way
she lets me idle in the brilliant drift.

FIVE WEDDING SONGS

i

Farewell long sweet night of my childhood!
flower heart I unpetaled for the sad bride
who wept, exhausted while the old Carpathian men
threw their silver dollars down onto the sawdust,
who catcalled her new name . . . *Mrs. Mrs.*
her old name lost inside her father's heart.
Her beauty *like the dome of heaven*
was built in a single frame and I heard her:

"It is time to go, groom
  sweep me up, out of here,
  to the north
  country of fur around the boots
  country of red blankets trimmed in black wool,
  house of tatted bedlinens & diamond windowpanes. . . ."

Leave her—

ii

This morning in Berkeley my mouth waters
as I walk past the Sari Palace, whose liquid
bolts embroider the walls, floor to ceiling,
and women are selecting cloth for love.
Someone spilled cobalt sequins on the sidewalk
hurrying home to sew her dress.
           I decide to follow
the constellation, a loose wash, stars falling
from red lips, my body is a satin page lifted forward
on a lingering night-thought, up

into the dustgold hills & their thin

stands of fir, temporary homes. Lost on a song, a trail,
bride of the daily, the diary,

I fashion this song
from the fleshy jade of eucalyptus,
from the blue flame of the air, & the sliding waters
of silk unfolded on wood.

iii

I lay in the green boat green
bottles chilled in the cooler. Away
on the wind birds left us, trees moved
framing us along the grey-blue surface unzipped
by the bow & the slicing of the oars as he pushed
down through the water. The dripping off the
end-curves of the wood wonderful as he rowed.
When we lit the lantern I heard the loon
and felt my face with my hands.
These bones, I said to myself, this face
will lie down next to his face.

iv

A month by the sea
feeds our sea-shack lone-
liness, delicious salt
laces the edges of our jeans

A month by the sea
breathes us into the slant-
sigh of the waves
a couple of times a day

A month by the sea
walks us into town at night
when the surf is out
and so are the fishers
tossing their lines by the light
of cedar-smoke fires
A month by the sea

turns us headfirst to the winds
in our jackets & jeans
& red wool socks
That is all we need
                    & a little
poetry, a little wine,
                    & something crackling
on the maritime radio.

                              v.

She married ink, she married water,
who was she? Look down
by the river, the blue bench barely
blue anymore, the wood polished
to wet wind stilled. There's a note taped
underneath and inside a piece of her wedding cloth
stitched with looking-glass. Place it on her grave
if you find her.

THE ICE FALL

Until they plow and salt the avenues
the city is hushed, everything's on delay

except the wristwatch of the EMT driver
who is out looking for the right house, and the snow

that isn't stopping, it's free,
and I'm taking off too

down the long low glide of meadow,
sunstruck & clear after the heavy storm

down to the edge of the brook
making its wet slate run through

the tiny canyon of Frick Park,
wind is rushing through the world

and I am asking
where is my love? In a snowbank

of sleep, snoring, Hi darling,
I left new work to show you,

it's on the table beside the milk.
No, dreamer, that is only a dream.

I hear an ambulance and swear I smell
a baker's truck wobbling up there

between drifts the size of Greenland—
(everything's bigger after the storm)

—where the snow is 120,000 years old,
snow that fell on Eric the Red

still intact. A Danish scientist right now
is hauling a sliver-layer of it back up,

snow that fell on the snowhouse
of an ancient mother who nursed

her screaming infant or let it suck
on seal fat. Down here in the woods

I have time to write a quick message
in maple syrup on the snow

then pick it up and eat it
or save it in an ice pack in my car

and give it to Margie, who will already
be at her screen, but I'm not going in

this morning; it's too beautiful & cold.
My nephews will be skiing on Utah

powder when they wake up, and if
they check their email they'll know

that here in the old country we are
happy, very happy with this storm

that threatens nothing but time
& the truly old, shut in & worried

but there's a topaz window
behind the clouds, it's the snow-sun

topaz, topkapi, love
is written there with all the other

jewels. I like a simple votive,
carpenter's candle in a jelly jar,

fire in a glass, a heating windshield
thawing against the burnishing white.

I want to run away so I am,
but not far, just here

walking down & along the spinning
rushing habitat of the brook,

its acoustics magnified against the canyon
wall, a wind-through-bells sound running along under

the Parkway and under Forbes and
it keeps moving at the speed of sound

and in one wild leap I'm across the water
and coming closer to the fall, the city has hundreds of them

but none with chins & eyebrows like these
resting on the heavy hemlocks sticking out

and sprung downward from the roughages
of the rocks. The mighty icicles aren't ready

to release drops into the brook, they're
sturdy & hard as a Mt. Rushmore of elvish

proportion rimming the water,
give me one more quick leap and one shaking

step and we're face to face. In a month
the icicles will melt into spring, all their pleated

thin wet ice-glass at the edges will be gone.
For now the fall's bulk is maybe a half foot thick,

though the white ice makes me nervous, could be rotten,
airpockets all through it. Try to climb that

and you'd crash down through chips & ice-shrapnel
everywhere, chunks the size of dinner plates. My boot

at the thinnest panel hits an edge and little
shards tumble down like pieces of glass

falling, or broken wind chimes, it's a nice
sound. Maybe I thought love could

open anything, I thought it was blue, color
of absolute happiness; I know it's solid & deep,

color of the most beautiful waterfalls
in winter, you can see blue depth like looking

into a marble or solid piece of colored glass.
They say love gets better over time, and the words

we say: *Have you ever felt* this *way?* release the one
word that comes astonishingly back from the beloved:

No, and that sweetest *no* is really an avalanche of *Yeses*.
as in "You make me feel yes to the infinity, yes

I've fallen, but now I'm falling deeper."
I hold my breath and I'm behind

the wall. We looked for petroglyphs
here, we looked for arrowheads & footprints,

fire-cracked rocks, shards, bottles with feathers
inside them. We looked for red or sulfur-colored

clay drawings of bear, deer, we looked
for any possible sign

of people come before. And we walked. We
walked behind the fall, we walked a snake line

we made ourselves fit the shapes of the slightest
pockets, this was our secret devotion: shift into

the quiet, don't touch the icicles,
they'll crash down, knock your eye out, give

you away to whomever might be looking
from out there. And what did we see?

—the bluest parts, the thickest
panels shut the outside world out

and sometimes in the inch-wide breaks we drew in
cold air like a drug, and the blue sky

reflected Earth's mind,
but we were its eyes. Through the thinnest

draperies we scanned the opposite side
of the canyon, all the layers of shale & sandstone

displayed their crooked geometries back at us
as if to say *We see you, we're on the lookout*

don't worry! You can
build a campfire behind the wall

and the heat will cause only the slightest sheen
of icemelt, a satin-thin wetness

one can drink like fine wine after enough of it
runs down in crystal strands into a jug. You can sleep and dream

there, in the firelit insulation of the cave
where love is.